ULTIMATE CAR BATTLES

ALFA ROMEO vs. MASERATI

Colin Crum

WINDMILL
BOOKS

New York

Published in 2014 by Windmill Books, An Imprint of Rosen Publishing
29 East 21st Street, New York, NY 10010

First Edition

Produced for Windmill by Cyan Candy, LLC
Designer: Erica Clendening, Cyan Candy
Editor for Windmill: Joshua Shadowens

Photo Credits: Cover (top), p. 24 Fedor Selivanov/Shutterstock.com; cover (bottom) Alexander
Chaikin/Shutterstock.com; p. 4 Evren Kalinbacak/Shutterstock.com; p. 5 Dikiiy/Shutterstock.
com; p. 6 E.peiffer@gmx.net, via Wikimedia Commons; pp. 7, 8, 12, 13, 16, 22 Wikimedia
Commons; p. 9 http://www.flickr.com/photos/49525325@N00/2744132897/, via Wikimedia
Commons; p. 10 www.traumautoarchiv.de, via Wikimedia Commons; p. 11 Simon Davison, via
Wikimedia Commons; p. 12 (top) http://content.uniquehomes.com/wp-content/uploads/2011/11/
four-of-the-Maseratibrothers.Jpg, via Wikimedia Commons; p. 14 Radoslaw Lecyk/Shutterstock.
com; pp. 15, 17 Brian Snelson, via Wikimedia Commons; p. 18 Stuart Elflett/Shutterstock.com;
p. 19 Philip Lange/Shutterstock.com; p. 20 Martin Lehmann/Shutterstock.com; p. 21 Michael
Stokes/Shutterstock.com; p. 23 David Merrett, via Wikimedia Commons; p. 25 Stefan Ataman/
Shutterstock.com; p. 26 David Villarreal Fernández, via Wikimedia Commons; pp. 27, 30 (top)
Darren Brode/Shutterstock.com; p. 30 (bottom) eans/Shutterstock.com.

Publisher Cataloging Data

Crum, Colin.
Alfa Romeo vs. Maserati / by Colin Crum. — First edition.
p. cm. — (Ultimate car battles)
Includes index.
ISBN 978-1-4777-9019-9 (library binding) — ISBN 978-1-4777-9020-5 (pbk.) —
ISBN 978-1-4777-9021-2 (6-pack)
1. Alfa Romeo automobile — Juvenile literature. 2. Maserati automobiles — Juvenile literature.
I. Crum, Colin. II. Title.
TL215.A35 C78 2014
629.222—d23

Manufactured in the United States of America

CPSIA Compliance Information: Batch #BW14WM: For Further Information contact Windmill Books, New York, New York at 1-866-478-0556

TABLE OF CONTENTS

FAST AND BEAUTIFUL

Since the early days of the automobile, Italy has been famous for its **luxury** sports cars and superfast racecars. Two of the oldest Italian companies known for designing stylish, speedy cars are Alfa Romeo and Maserati.

Both companies have been around for more than 100 years!

Today, Alfa Romeo and Maserati both make cars that are fast, beautiful, and expensive. However, Alfa Romeos are designed to be

2013 Maserati GranTurismo

This is the 2009 Alfa Romeo 8C Spider. Just 500 of these convertibles were built. The 8C Spider has a top speed of 180 miles per hour (290 km/h)!

sportier than Maseratis. This means their focus is on speed, power, and **handling**. Maserati is better known for making luxury car models. They design cars with comfort, style, and special features in mind.

For a long time, Alfa Romeo and Maserati were **rivals** on and off the racetrack! Today, they are both owned by Fiat. Some people love sporty Alfa Romeos, while others love the luxury of Maserati!

ALL ABOUT ALFA ROMEO

Alfa Romeo's cars have always had a sporty feel. From the beginning, Alfa Romeo made fast road cars and even faster racecars. In fact, famous racer Enzo Ferrari got his start as an Alfa Romeo driver.

One of the most famous Alfa Romeo cars is the Spider Duetto. This classic convertible appeared in the 1967 movie *The Graduate*, starring Dustin Hoffman.

Here you can see a 1966 Spider Duetto. This convertible was designed by a famous Italian car design, Pininfarina. Pininfarina has designed many Italian sports cars, including Ferraris and Maseratis.

3317 ZG 54

Alfa Romeo Logo

In the United States, Alfa Romeos are somewhat rare. This is because Alfa Romeo stopped **exporting** to the United States in 1995. However, 500 brand new 4C **coupes** will be sold in the United States in 2014. Alfa Romeo plans to export more models soon!

Alfa Romeo's Logo

The Alfa Romeo logo, or badge, is a circle split into two parts. On the left side is a red cross on a white background. On the right side is a green snake wearing a crown. These two symbols are linked to the history of Milan, Italy, where Alfa Romeo was founded.

GETTING TO KNOW MASERATI

When many people think of Maserati, they think of car racing. Between the 1920s and late 1950s, Maserati was famous for making powerful racecars with many wins. Today, Maserati is known mostly for its small line of super luxury sports cars and **sedans**.

Maseratis stand out from other cars with their extra large **radiator grilles**. Over the years, the grille has changed shape from an oval to a rounded rectangle.

Maserati Grille

MASERATI

Maserati Logo

The MC12 supercar, shown here, was introduced in 2004. A supercar is a very fast, very expensive sports car. The MC12 can reach a top speed of 205 miles per hour (330 km/h).

One of the rarest Maseratis of all time is the MC12 supercar. Originally built for racing, just 50 MC12s were built to be legal for street driving. These MC12s sold for more than $700,000 each in the United States!

Maserati's Logo

Maserati's logo is a three-pronged spear, or trident. The trident is the symbol of the Roman god of the sea, Neptune. There is a statue of Neptune holding a trident in a fountain in Bologna, Italy. The Maserati brothers grew up in Bologna. Mario Maserati designed the trident logo with the fountain in mind.

ALFA ROMEO'S BEGINNINGS

Alfa Romeo started out as a company called ALFA. ALFA was founded near Milan, Italy in 1910. ALFA's first road car was the 1910 24 HP. It had a top speed of 60 miles per hour (97 km/h). ALFA made its first racecar, the Corsa, in 1911. In 1920, ALFA changed its name to Alfa Romeo. The first car called an Alfa Romeo was the 1920 Torpedo 20-20 HP.

Throughout the 1920s and 1930s, Alfa Romeo became

This is ALFA's first car, the 1910 24 HP. This car was built with a 4-**cylinder** engine and single-shaft transmission. About 300 24 HPs were built between 1910 and 1913.

The 8C 2900 roadster, shown here, was designed for racing. Scuderia Ferrari, Enzo Ferrari's racing team, drove Alfa Romeo 8C 2900s in the 1936 and 1937 Mille Miglia races.

known for its racing wins. They improved performance with each new racecar or sports car. The 6C 2500, made between 1938 and 1952, was known for being beautiful and super expensive.

In 1950, Alfa Romeo showed the 1900 sports sedan at the Paris Motor Show. This was the first Alfa Romeo built on a **production line**.

THE START OF MASERATI

Maserati was founded by Alfieri Maserati and five of his brothers in Bologna, Italy in 1914. The Maserati brothers were known for designing and racing cars for other companies. However, they wanted to build cars of their own.

The first car with the Maserati name was built in 1926. This racecar was called the Tipo 26. Alfieri drove the Tipo 26 in a road race called the Targa Florio. The Tipo 26 won first in its class! The Maserati brothers worked on

Left: Four of the Maserati brothers stand in front their company building near Bologna, Italy. Below: Here, a Maserati racecar speeds down the AVUS racetrack in Berlin, Germany in 1931.

This is a 1957 Maserati 200SI two-seater racecar. This car's smooth aluminum body was designed to be very **aerodynamic**. The 200SI was built with no roof and no doors!

building engines with more and more cylinders.

Until the 1950s, Maserati stayed focused on designing winning racing cars with powerful engines. In 1957,

Maserati retired from team racing. They shifted to selling cars for the road. In 1958, Maserati introduced their first large-scale production model, the beautiful 3500 GT coupe.

CHANGES FOR ALFA ROMEO

In 1954, Alfa Romeo introduced the small and sporty Giuletta. The Giuletta quickly became one of Alfa Romeo's most popular models. Drivers loved the car's style and performance.

In 1960, Alfa Romeo built a factory and began large-scale production.

The Giulia sports sedan was introduced in 1962. Many different versions of the Giulia were made, including the

1957 Giulia
Sprint Speciale

Spring GT, TZ, and the Spider Duetto. Between 1962 and 1978, more than 1 million Giulias were built.

In 1970, the Montreal sports car went into production. It was built with 200-**horsepower** V8 engine that could reach 135 miles per hour (217 km/h). The Montreal was more expensive than a Jaguar E-Type or Porsche 911!

Alfa Romeo 33.2 Concept

Alfa Romeo introduced the 33.2 *concept car* at the Paris Motor Show in 1969. This concept was a futuristic redesign of the 33 Stradale with a super aerodynamic shape. The bright yellow 33.2 was built with a V8 engine and could go 160 miles per hour (258 km/h). It also featured butterfly doors and pop-up headlights.

MASERATI OVER TIME

In 1963, Maserati introduced their first four-door sedan, the Quattroporte. The Quattroporte had a top speed of more than 120 miles per hour (193 km/h). The super popular 1967 Maserati Ghibli coupe was built with a V8 engine. The Ghibli could go from 0 to 60 miles (0–97 km/h) per hour in 6.8 seconds. A French company called Citroen bought Maserati in 1968.

In the 1970s, Maserati built many popular models. These

This is a 1973 Maserati Bora supercar. The Bora was a two-seat coupe with a mid-engine layout. It was built with a 4.9-liter V8 engine that could make 310 horsepower.

Maserati Merak

included the high-performance Bora supercar, the Merak sports car, and the low, flat Khamsin sports car.

After another change in ownership, Fiat bought Maserati in 1993. Then, they put Ferrari in charge of Maserati in 1997.

Maserati and Ferrari

Under Ferrari's ownership, Maserati was made into a true luxury car brand. The luxury 3200 GT coupe was introduced in 1998. The Maserati Coupe and Spyder were the first Maseratis sold in the United States in 11 years. In 2002, Ferrari introduced the new Maserati Quattroporte line designed by Pininfarina.

ALFA ROMEO IN RACING

Over the years, Alfa Romeo has had success in nearly every kind of car racing. This includes Grand Prix racing, sports car racing, and touring car racing.

The 1920s and 1930s were the golden years of Alfa Romeo racing. In this time, Alfa Romeo became incredibly famous for their racing wins. Between 1928 and 1947,

Over the years, Alfa Romeo has also made and sold racing engines. For example, this Dallara F301 Formula Three racecar is powered by an Alfa Romeo engine.

This is a 1950 Alfa Romeo Tipo 159 racecar. The Tipo 159 was built for the 1951 Formula One season. Part of this model's body has been removed to show its engine.

drivers racing Alfa Romeos won the Mille Miglia race 11 times. Winning racecar models included the 6C 1500 Sport Spider Zagato and the Alfa Romeo 8C 2900 Tipo B. Alfa Romeo 8C 2300 racers won the 24 Hours of Le Mans endurance race four years in a row, between 1931 and 1934.

Beginning in the 1960s, Alfa Romeo has competed in the European Touring Car Championships with 17 wins. Most recently, Alfa Romeo 156 racers won every year between 2000 and 2003.

MASERATI IN MOTORSPORTS

Like Alfa Romeo, Maserati had success in many different kinds of car racing. This includes Grand Prix racing, sports car racing, endurance racing, and Formula One racing.

Before World War II, Maserati was hard at work building racecars with powerful engines for Grand Prix racing. They even designed a model called the 4V with a 16-cylinder engine! A racer named Wilbur Shaw won the Indy 500 race driving a Maserati 8CTF in 1939 and 1940.

Here, a driver takes part in a vintage car race with a 1933 Maserati 8CM one-seat formula racecar. A Maserati 8CM won the Belgian Grand Prix in 1933.

This is a Maserati Tipo 61 Birdcage sports car racer, built between 1959 and 1961. This car could make 250 horsepower and had a top speed of 177 miles per hour (285 km/h).

Maserati took part in Formula One racing from the 1940s to the 1960s. During this time, Maserati had 9 Grand Prix wins and one driver's world championship title. Maserati built three different Formula One racer models. These were the Maserati 4CLT, the Maserati A6GCM, and the Maserati 250F. Maserati also took wins in World Sportscar Championship races in the 1950s and 1960s.

TARGA FLORIO RIVALS

Alfa Romeo and Maserati were racing rivals in the 1930s. At this time, both companies were focused on building fast racers with powerful engines. One of their greatest rivalries took place at the Targa Florio road race in Sicily, Italy.

Alfa Romeo 8C 2300 Monza

Maserati 6CM

Alfa Romeo became super famous for winning the Targa Florio road race for six years in a row starting in 1930. Winning Alfa Romeo racecars included the P2, the 8C 2300 Monza, and the Tipo B P3. However, when Maserati introduced the 6CM at the 1937 Targa Florio, Alfa Romeo could not compete! Maserati racers won for four years in a row, between 1937 and 1940.

Single-seat Racecars

The Alfa Romeo Tipo B P3 and Maserati 6CM were both single-seat racecars with wheels built outside their bodies. This kind of car is sometimes called a formula racecar. They are designed for racing at high speeds for long distances. Both cars had a top speed of about 140 miles per hour (225 km/h)!

THE FUTURE FOR ALFA ROMEO

Alfa Romeo has been owned by Fiat since 1986. Today, Alfa Romeo has a small range of sporty cars. The MiTo, introduced in 2008, is a three-door minicar. The Giuletta, first shown in 2010, is a small family car. In 2013, the 4C two-seater coupe went into production. The 4C is small, lightweight, and features rear-wheel drive.

Alfa Romeo has many plans for the future. An updated

Here, the Alfa Romeo 4C concept is shown at the 2011 Geneva Motor Show in Geneva, Switzerland. The 4C is an example of a concept car that was put into production!

Alfa Romeo MiTo

Giulia sedan may be in development, as well as a new Spider convertible. Alfa Romeo may also be working on a sport utility vehicle based on a Jeep body design. Look for these new Alfa Romeos soon!

Gloria Concept Car

Alfa Romeo introduced a concept for a new sports sedan at the 2013 Geneva Auto Show. This concept car is called the Gloria. The Gloria was designed by the European Design Institute of Turin. It is small and angular with **LED** slots for headlights. This concept car looks very different than current Alfa Romeo models!

WHAT'S NEXT FOR MASERATI?

In 2005, Fiat took control of Maserati. Today, Maserati offers a small range of luxury cars. The sixth-generation Quattroporte was introduced in 2013. This sedan features V6 or V8 engines built by Ferrari.

Maserati also introduced a smaller sedan, the Ghibli, at the Shanghai Motor Show, in 2013. The GranTurismo is a grand-tourer, while the GranCabrio is a convertible version of the GranTurismo.

Maserati showed a concept for a luxury sport utility vehicle at the 2011 Frankfurt Auto Show. This SUV concept was called the Maserati Kubang.

MASERATI

Maserati also has plans for a luxury sport utility vehicle. This SUV may be called the Kubang or the Levante. Maserati hopes their SUV will compete against other luxury SUVs such as the BMW X5 M and the Porsche Cayenne.

Birdcage 75th Concept Car

One of Maserati's most famous concept cars is the futuristic Birdcage 75th. This car was designed by Pininfarina in 2005 to celebrate its 75th **anniversary**. The Birdcage 75th does not have doors. Instead, part of its body raises up for a driver to climb in. This is called a bubble canopy.

COMPARING CARS

For a long time, Alfa Romeo and Maserati were rivals! Today, both brands are owned by the same company. However, Alfa

ALFA ROMEO

Date Founded	1910 (as ALFA)
First Model	1910 24 HP
Current Owner	Fiat Group
Headquarters	Turin, Italy
Current Models in 2013–2014	MiTo Giuletta 4C
Best 0–60 mph (0–97 km/h)	2011 TZ3 Stradale Zagato 3.5 seconds
Top Speed	2011 TZ3 Stradale Zagato 199 miles per hour (320 km/h)
Most Powerful Engine	2011 TZ3 Stradale Zagato 8.4-liter V10 engine 640 HP
Cars Sold, 2012	101,000

Romeo and Maserati are still competing for customers. If you compare Alfa Romeo and Maserati over time, you will see many similarities. You will also see some differences!

MASERATI

Date Founded	1914
First Model	1926 Tipo 26
Current Owner	Fiat Group
Headquarters	Modena, Italy
Current Models in 2013–2014	Quattroporte Ghibli GranTurismo GranCabrio
Best 0–60 mph (0–97 km/h)	2004 MC12 3.7 seconds
Top Speed	2004 MC12 205 miles per hour (330 km/h)
Most Powerful Engine	2011 Gran Turismo MC Stradale Novitec Tridente 4.7-liter V8 engine 646 HP
Cars Sold, 2012	6,288

YOU DECIDE!

Alfa Romeo and Maserati have been through many changes over the years. For many years, they were racetrack rivals! They also battled to design the best high-performance Italian sports car.

Today, Alfa Romeo and Maserati make up Fiat's sports and luxury division. While Maserati focuses on luxury, Alfa Romeo designs cars with a sporty feel. However, both companies work together to share parts, technologies, and production.

Which do you like better, sporty Alfa Romeo or luxurious Maserati? Only you can decide!

Alfa Romeo 8C Competizione

Maserati GranCabrio Sport

GLOSSARY

aerodynamic (er-oh-dy-NA-mik) Made to move through the air easily.

anniversary (a-nuh-VURS-ree) The date on which an event occurred in the past or its special observance.

concept car (KON-sept KAR) A car to show new features and technology.

coupes (KOOPS) Cars with two doors and a hard roof.

cylinder (SIH-lun-dur) The enclosed space for a piston in an engine.

exporting (EK-spor-ting) Sending good or services to another country for sale.

handling (HAND-ling) Stability while driving an automobile, such as cornering and swerving.

horsepower (HORS-pow-ur) The way an engine's power is measured. One horsepower is the power to lift 550 pounds (250 kg) 1 foot (.3 m) in 1 second.

LED (el-ee-DEE) A semiconductor light source.

luxury (LUK-shuh-ree) Comforts and beauties of life that are not necessary.

production line (pruh-DUK-shun LYN) A system in which a product is made by being moved down a line of workers and machines that complete different steps.

radiator grilles (RAY-dee-ay-tur GRILZ) Grated covers that allow air in to cool the car's radiator.

rivals (RY-vulz) People or companies who try to beat others at something.

sedans (suh-DANZ) Cars that seat four or more people.

FURTHER READING

Power, Bob. *Maseratis*. Wild Wheels. New York: Gareth Stevens Learning Library, 2011.

Quinlan, Julia J. *Alfa Romeo*. Speed Machines. New York: PowerKids Press, 2012.

Schaefer, A.R. *Maserati*. Fast Cars. Mankato, MN: Capstone Press, 2008.

INDEX

WEBSITES

For web resources related to the subject of this book, go to:
www.windmillbooks.com/weblinks
and select this book's title.